Bone Harvest Done

Poems

John Fairfax

Sidgwick & Jackson
London

For Esther, Michael and Jonathan

First published in Great Britain in 1980
by Sidgwick & Jackson Limited
Copyright © John Fairfax 1980
ISBN 0 283 98626 3
Printed in Great Britain by
T. & A. Constable Ltd, Edinburgh
for Sidgwick & Jackson Limited
1 Tavistock Chambers, Bloomsbury Way
London WC1A 2SG

Contents

Fantasy for a Child	1
We move under the dust and breath of stars	3
We are Three	4
If Death be Dark	5
Tiger Hunter	6
A Bullet at Millau	8
A Boy and a Rabbit	10
A Stream Recalled	11
Prelude for Michael	13
For Jonathan	14
For Elsbeth Merlin Moat	15
The Story	16
December on the Downs	17
Remembering	18
Three Swallows	19
At a Seawall	20
Lines for Esther, August 30	21
A Logfire	22
Bone Harvest Done	23
Badgerskin	25
February Morning	27
I cannot shout that the lyric lie decayed	28
Star Spurred	29
Stages from a Lamenting Tongue	31
Five songs	
Moonsong	35
Song of the Wind	36
Liberty Track	37
Mountains Sing	37
My Love come and join Me	38
The Anchorage	39
Wendy Anne Mitchell	40
Lines from Wales	41

Elan Valley	42
At the Glen of Drumtochty	43
The Zennor Road	44
April Mooned	45
Beyond Astronaut	46
Columbus of the Sky	47
The Sea of Tranquillity	48
Space Walk	50
12 Stations from Gemini	51
Adrift on the Star Brow of Taliesin	54

Acknowledgement is due to the editors of the following:
Outposts; Panache; Paris Review; Poetry Review; Spectator; Time and Tide; Times Literary Supplement; Two Cities; and the BBC 3rd programme which broadcast 'Badgerskin', 'February Morning', 'Wendy Anne Mitchell'.

Fantasy for a Child

I remember a track between the trees
My ash stick that cut down the thorn
And sliced the gold-headed flowers,
And moved a stone beneath the water
Of a stream I remember now:
Against a ruined wall and broken tree
I remember those bubbling years.

Companions never lost their way.
I remember following the moon to the sea
Down a corridor of boulders and night,
My hair grasped by the hard hand of an oak;
I remember, and so do they.

I remember a flight across the land –
Whether a dream or mine.
I remember the waiting: and commands
That ran like water in my ears.
I remember fishing from a boat.

I walked with the trees and sun,
With my ash stick and my laughter
Away from the market and the noise
Of tears, and business that was not mine.
I remember the motionless air and am glad.

I remember a grove and sleeping friends
And night, flames, feeling like thieves
And hanging like them in the shadows,
Until I became one and was caught
Beneath the trees because friends slept.

I remember the ash stick and the thorns,
Green thorns whirling from a hedge
And flowers falling golden on the grass.
I remember a summer of birds and sky of trees
That have died and now die with me.

We move under the dust and breath of stars

We move under the dust and breath of stars
And accompany bright widows in tears,
And unravel the winding clothes that shield
The three tombed kings whose courtiers die
Daily and lie in immortality.

Under the oak, under the gorse and grass,
Under sand, from pools of death they come
Bearing gifts,
Recognising river and place of birth
Reaching to the hand that lifts the lid
And salutes from a birth and death ago.

Late winter lambs and remaining birds prance
To the re-echoed beats that pulse the day
Each king and each child takes up the song.
It is not death, where we died
Yielding in the arms of earth and sleep.
The mutes speak out of their bones and movement,
Boughs gesture and the sea sculps rock
While we move and our hands are not empty
But bounding from a life and from a tomb.

We are Three

Guess.   That trailing mark is written
Above every cot before the child is there,
Bells ring and candles light the to-bed stairs.
A storm, closed, hand in glove,
Quails under dividing hands, and is conveyed
From Orion's belt and from the plough,
From the little sister at the telephone,
Caesars in Cleopatra beds, spaniels
With celtic eyes, and from kittens with wool.
Quail, wisemen, there the proverb plays.
Bright mouth on my sore shoulder.   Sleep.

I dream my time away, and watch
The fishes among watergrass and birds
Among a sky of trees, animals among themselves,
And all that move and can be watched.
But mostly I dream.   The words
Follow.   The grief is there.   It is
Blossoming to a death.   Hands, feet and head
Deep in the grave.   But that question
Repeats: We are three, we are three?
Resounding like a silence in every ear.

If Death be Dark
To remember Siegfried Sassoon

Is all lost just left behind to grumble
In a cobwebbed room full of notebooks,
Brown photographs and half remembered things?

We begin to make a block of memory to span
From bricabrac to newly treasured junk,
Our youth compressed behind a stretching mask.

A landscape then is now a distance mapping
A hurt healed or love exploding into words.
Framed features or lock of hair is all that's left

Of friends we pledged.   A trinket lost in passing
Has its place beneath the skin of our rising day.
Names and words we knew then are no longer sharp.

Each face, memory, word, thrown back collects
A shield of difference.   Deceit and dust
To shield from dark death what we cannot bear.

Tiger Hunter

After reading 'Man-eaters of Kumaon'
by Jim Corbett

For T. H.

A bolt
Of instinct released
The white hunter
Whose red and yellow tiger brain
Iced his predatory blood
Gliding his limbs
Over telltale spoor.

The white hunter
tacked along the wind,
No noise of tumbling stone
No breaking twig.
The tiger is hunter enough
In ten foot of tooth and claw.
Hunters hunger for the air of each other.

The man
Moves to the nerve caution
Of his hide as though outlines
In his brain were cast by tiger growl.
They are both still.
Waiting, sniffing the wind,
Turning, turning, half turning,
Back and forward

Until the earth is thick
With track and scent.
Bird, monkey, and stag
Cease their calling
In full throated fear
So red is the bursting spell
Filling the sky from that great head.

Pad and boot, boot and pad,
Over and over
As the tongue dries on teeth
And eyes pierce leaf and thorn
Priming his body
And brain to kill or die:
Man to tiger. Tiger to man

Drawing pictures in the sand –
Scratch marks of flexing claw,
Rifle butt and scuffing toe.
Tighter and tighter
The circling
Until a stopped heart of bullet-break
Or claw-strike explodes

A sinewed minute
Of hunter and hunter.
The ten foot tiger
Arches no more for man's carcass
And sweet blood
A worming bullet splinters
All memory from his head.

A Bullet at Millau
For Hal

Their canopies crack open
Both paratroopers drop

              Cord and webbing, feet together,
              Through different air.

One needs to die
The other lives to die.

              At the practice range
              A single bullet links them.

Thirty yards apart one's intent
Invisibly checks the other's track.

              A trooper watches the target
              As he butterflies an idle day.

Inside one skull a knot tightens:
He cannot wait to die.

              A trooper lights a gauloises
              Setting tomorrow aglow.

From his skull's blackhole
One shrinks in his jumpjacket.

              Wall eyed one no longer sees,
              His fingers fondle his rifle.

A trooper looks right and left
A shadow blinks his right eye.

                The other, thirty yards away
                Raises his rifle to his chest.

A paratrooper stands.   Bound.
A shadow jumps.   Cracks open.   Passes.

                He squeezes the trigger
                The shadow must escape.

He feels the sun unzip his jacket
And waits to hear his chute flower.

                Under a stud of one left pocket
                The green and brown flows red.

Across both men one falling bullet
Has hooked them on to death.

A Boy and a Rabbit

Running as untamed as the sky
Along highways of grass a rabbit,
Halted by a poacher's ring, was killed.
The poacher, a boy unknown to death,
Saw his own road gold with traps.
Watching his prey's dead eyes,
With questions transfixed for reply,
The boy crying at his power
Took the rabbit home and lay
That death on a board. He drew the figure
Answering its eyes and head
In the colour of his defeat.

A Stream Recalled

Steps from my childhood led
To a flagstone corridor –
Distorting mirror.
The corridor sloped
Steeply enough
For toys to race down.

The flagstones were cold blue.
Sometimes they sang.

In winter they hissed, and a rime
Shimmered along the corridor.
Those days I hurried through the place
To warm rooms.
Each day sealed its temper on me
Echoing my heel tap.

Beneath the stones on summer days
There were finger bells
That teased me to kneel and listen
Until into my head that stream,
Under the hallway of my boyhood,
Etched deep runs.
Even now I hear it when I listen.

I remember one room in
The house was silent.
That was my parents' room.
I barely knew it – the quiet
Was its lock.

They are fixed behind the mirror
Of that childhood
By their separate stairway,
Dark door;
Their tall and hollow room.

They could not read
The flagstones
Nor dream the corridor
Nor hear my Devon stream.

Once I clambered rocks of returning
To find only blue flagstones
Bridging a stream below a hallway.

Yet I think I know the shadow
I caught kneeling to hear the water.
I see a boy listen when I listen.

Prelude for Michael

March in the mad Spring from my cottage
Sped and touched eyehills with a blackened hand.
Come, Michael, beside our tall, tall fir,
Spread your three years over a spell as fast
As the beaten babes kissed by winter.
What your inheritance I cannot guess.

A moth like time beats at the window
That you must ride master out all your days.
Michael, draw your bow and kiss the gut.
Be sure. Loose the bolt and pin the gold.
Welcome your days with a memory
Of unlikely Pentecosts. Michael remember

March is mad, seasons are your margin.
Armour yourself for war with a fistful
Of dreaming dust always in the hand,
Both false and flourishing. Come, Michael,
Here by our cottage. It was here we talked
Of invisible one, and what will be.

For Jonathan

Down, down the bright slide of day
The enlarging sun careers
Through geographies. And, at last,
Bled crimson, rests
Beneath the hills, beyond the woods
Where only you, my babe, shall play.

For Elsbeth Merlin Moat

The valley breathes a lullaby
Bamboo and medlar take up
The theme as water silvers
Across blue stone
Gently not to waken you.

From wishes into dreams you grow,
As doves circle above your cot
And dogs curl by your door,
To hold the valley
Entranced in your sleeping eye.

Song fill your waking, prayer your sleep.
O child it is a summer
Promise that lies beside you
Blossoming gold
In the seasons of childhood.

So keenly will his eye observe
All detail of your growing
And softly her hand caress
Away grief and pain
As you grow into their landscape.

The Story

Find that tomb
Where our kin
Rest their swords
Till we beat
The alarm.
And all people
Must shoulder
Father to son,
Son to father.
Prince of the house
And Jack rise,
Saddle and ride
Down the ranks.

December on the Downs

A December day I walked upon the Downs
And watched the hares curvet and crows
Curl on the wind. My sons kicked
Tufts of grass and ran the mud
Along their boots, each with his hood
Pulled tight against a northern wind.
Our voices were cut from our mouths
And word and laugh lost across the hills.

We broke the ice from rutted pools
And traced frozen footprints of a fox
And pheasant as the ice melted in our hands.
The sun, white and low, and snow flurried
Onto the flattened grass. Two riders
Raised their arms in greeting, horses bobbed,
And my sons called out, but the snow
Hid the greeting and the horsemen were gone.

We reached the ridgeway atop a hill
And pushed against the wind to a temple
That once kept Roman gods over this land.
Each son climbed a knoll and surveyed
The valley on either side. They called homage
Before we left. I led from the ridgeway
So that through twilight the wind
At our backs rode us home.

Remembering

Yesterday is my tomorrow
And I breathe deep before blood
Runs cold and my eyes turn
Deeply inward. I remember long
Limbed girl with midnight hair.

I sang roistering lads
To silence and my knife was keen
As the wayfaring names I ran
For love and lust and blazing bone.

Yesterday is my tomorrow.

I recall voyages, the wine
Brimmed with pictures and young love
Then did I set out with resolve
Over plain and up harsh valley.

But that was when this Headland
Was dim in the landscape of my skull,
And until I heard a blind singer
Hum a beacon. Calling. Calling me

Yesterday is my tomorrow
Calling, calling me.

Three Swallows

They came late
  three of them
stitching holes in
  the summer air.
An equinox shivered
  above the bee-
laden buddlia.

Early summer
  the bees had it
their way sucking
  out the golden
baubles of July:
  hiving a clear
run between
  nectar and cell.

Minutes tally
  each latitude,
divided hemispheres
  pilot swallows
whose auguries
  turn seasons
into flight.

The air awoke
  alive to swallows
drawing a fine net
  of sky down
toward full rose,
  columbine, bramble,
and setting apple.

Over the thatch
  and buddlia
three swallows rake
  honey heavy bees
in a summer haul.
  From my shed
three swallows
  punctuate my summer.

At a Seawall

Tonight alone at a seawall
I hear her song
And the island spins.

She dances circles in the tide
which flows and falls combed
Through her hair.

She holds wave and breaker then pours
Them from her hand
To pearl the rock.

As night parts the battered stars
Catch the white hem
Of her frail dress.

Tonight alone at a seawall
I reach for her hand and the cry
Of gulls deafens me.

O I know her in white water,
In green sea, in storming water.
I know her touch.

She hums a rockabye
Picks chords on every surf
And frets the sand.

She sighs in depth and shallow,
Rages sea at fringed bay,
Blinds me with gazing.

Tonight alone at a seawall
The moon and I stare
While one awake cries.

The shore changes.   Seabirds ride
And feed alone on sea-surge.
She haunts my song.

She calls me but I cannot go.
I made this seawall
Where alone tonight I listen.

Lines for Esther, August 30

On each other we have sprung a decade of love;
And I see my sons among birch trees
Stretch from our bed.   We could not celebrate
In beer and meat our matrimonial day
For lack of cash, but my love, we have kicked
The backside of mortgage and loose
Couches for ten years which makes my verse
To you the ring we did not need of gold.

As I remember we joined on a wet day,
A chinese meal and a curtain ring.
Our beds have been bare but of our choice,
And you from tears to both sons had faith
When stolen food eased the boys' bellies.
Have this address of my love, Esther, which I know
You do not need in words as our love spills
Over verb and gift and grief of possession.

A Logfire

A geography of fire
Brands on an oak log,
Huge as a thigh,
Those enchanting shapes
From the barbary coast
That I see in the wood
Through prism of a tear
That dries on my cheek
As I dream before the blaze.

Bone Harvest Done

Speak: for who can say
Where the farthest star clings,
Or the sun unlooses day,
Or a dead blue Jay swings?

September covers summer
And flesh crawls under wool,
The sky, an insane drummer,
Beats down my winter fuel.

O speak: for who can say
Come with me? Who will give
Hand warmth to a child's play
Against nightmares that live?

Abed in unkicked leaves
The babes dress in their grief
And autumns, dark as thieves,
Make their comfort brief.

Bone harvest done: they swear
Death lasts. Be sure to die,
It is all you live to bear
Since broken hearts must lie.

O speak: for who can say
Where the farthest star clings
Or the sun unlooses day,
Or a dead blue Jay swings?

Live apace upon a hill,
Break against a northern wind,
Feel them turn on you to kill
Because you love: and love sinned.

A child in autumn sapped
And stretched a harvest hand
Full of words night lapped
For the bright wings that fanned

Before they died to hang
On a wire fence.   And you walk
Shouting at what dared to gang
Against you – sparrow riled hawk?

Sprinkle out, break or bow out,
Prettier than you were kicked
By the transparent lout
Flouncing the ones he picked

To wheel screeching gullwise
Over Nomansland.   Turn stone,
Shoulder sky, the dead disguise
Themselves in wind-white bone.

O speak: for who can say
Where the farthest star clings,
Or the sun unlooses day,
Or a dead blue Jay swings?

Badgerskin

A badger skin pinned by nails
To the creosote planks of a barn
Shrinks in the sun.   Mud dries
On the pads behind claws
So lately grubbing leaves and roots:
And strange geographies of blood
Print the hide with outlines
That can be read as easily
As the thinbladed knife
That severs skin from bone,
Or as easily as a gamekeeper's
Finger can load his gun
And triggerhook to defend
Pheasants' eggs he broods
Over with more anxiety
Than a hen.   The badger
Faltered: and now his pied skin,
Adorning a thatched shed,
Is held by fencing nails
As blood, nerves, and bone
Are cast into a hole
Scratched at by guineafowl.

The sun marks the three stars
In the skin that were eyes
And a bullet hole.   Like lace
The hide looks as death
Smells and shrinks from the nails.
This blurred cross high
On a wall is as much monument
As the tongue stone we fall under.
There is power in the badger pelt
Pinned like a lace mask
Of Cain on the gamekeeper's barn.

Those pads, with mud dried
To the delving claws, recently
Inhabited the wood
Behind my cottage where my boots
Receive mud covering, mind claws.
There are no eyes in the skin
For me to recognise glint
Of warning; but eyes deceive.
The holes in the lace are eyes,
The lace is skin, the nails
Are not in a cross;
But the night-and-day pelt
Is distinct as it yells
From the barn wall where it dries
In the sun and wind
Ignored by a killer with mud on his boots
Who protects pheasants' eggs
With long weapons and death.

February Morning

I dream through this winter of mist and gossamer.
Calm from the season engrosses my wood.
Spring is weeks away.

Magpie, crow and pheasant no longer stir the air
With harsh cry and frightened wing beating the wind.
A mist heavy with ice is adding frozen tracery
To sleeping limb of hazel, holly, laurel and beech.

As I walk over white brittle grass I hear
But cannot see bunched cattle scraping pasture,
Can hear distant ploughs turning iron furrows
Until the tractor stops and silence is full.

The wood I walk is close as the unmoving winter
Of this February morning. Down a rhododendron track
I pass with my hands warm in my pockets to where
A pheasant caught in a keeper's trap breaks the quiet
As she thrusts at the netting, losing feathers in fear.

In this black month the trap is harmless,
It is there to collect her to mother another brood
To feed next autumn sport. I go by and she settles
To eat the crop that trapped her.

                A grey squirrel
Perches on the bole of an oak taking no notice as I pass –
No screwing scamper along branches, no anxious leap –
It sits motionless. The people of Eling Wood and winter
Are thickblooded through this frozen morning.

Even late gossamer from bramble to bracken is unbroken;
And as I walk deeper among the trees I am affected
To move with care. With care I breathe and walk
As, I too, await the Spring.

I cannot shout that the lyric lie decayed

I cannot shout that the lyric lie decayed
On a latitude pursued by a spring moon,
Cannot silently shift my pen protesting
Against a frogthroated minstrel who is unwired
Without the skeleton of a harp.   Listen.
The rain objects, and the wind is out of tune,
The bee hums flat and the wasp is hopping mad
At the fugue flowers allow.   Lyric lie decay.

Today while I rested at my door I heard
An infant and an old man talking in verse.
This is spring when that may happen.
And it did.   And still the lyric lie decayed.
I did not see a brand of fire spit flame
At the sea nor did I see a mountain dance.
But this was a dream heart hung with my anger.
And as they walked on through the mouth of a hill
I followed, as though called by a pied player.
I do not say that the lyric lie decayed.

Star Spurred

The tale is told my words have gone
With wind and spindrift up along

The valley from the sea's dry line
To where like cinnamon brackens shine

At the moon's lowering eye
Softlanding tears of goodbye.

I'll hum no tune by water edge
Unless my love in silent pledge

Will know my flight is curling through
The warrens of her loving too;

And hold, although I must depart,
The broken measure of our heart.

As I look back so salt appears
Carving figures from my tears.

My ear picks at the rhyming of
A swinging gate or sleeping dove

And hears the water of the stream
Lulling a dragonfly to dream.

No matter from where nor how far
I'll chart the circle of my star

Back to this valley by the shore
To clasp the hand of love once more

And for a season of delight
Will flower a stillness in the night.

Stages from a Lamenting Tongue

1

Along a wordless parabola
I multiplied days
And found no escape:
Until a golden spur urged me
Headlong towards the moon
On a trajectory computed
In my pulse.

I drifted endless roads
And nameless towns
Until my flight was arrested.

An echo raged in my head.
No tongue could I find
For the thundering of my ears.

I came to the lap of an ocean
And my journey ended (and began).
I fingered a sea of tears
And laughter – a sea of chaos
And tranquillity.   There in dream I saw
My oarless coracle spinning.

2

Songs echoing from rock
Broke into my skull and against
My ribs shaking this frame
As though nothing but dry leaves
And moondust were alive in me.

By Atlantic water and hewn cliff,
By river and at the root of the oak,
In word-freezing air and snapping
Moonshafts, I have listened to song.

Then at last the sea sang.
A dog ran, a hand reached out,
The winds shifted in my ears
And words — heat shielded —
Dropped from my tongue
And their silence deafened me.

I grew in shadow
Until a blade of light
Burned at my lips
And I called your name
Down a history
Of anguished bone
To douse the pain.
Yet no rhythm could break
My silence.

3

I looked into the waters
Of each stone bridge I found
And watched the boulders move.
I felt a sword in my hand
Thrust and twist on bone.
I learned the cunning of the gull
In flight against wind and cliff.
I caught the dialogue of seasons
And counted each breath.
I was amazed as the head
Of Apollo floated in a red collar
On an Ocean .... calling.

The poets sang.   They heard and sang.
I saw a striped shroud mark
The bobbing skull.
Then I heard that death
Was all about: in every wavelength
In every calculation,
In every deed;
In the hand of love clasped
To the hand of love.

4

The first cold hand to clasp mine
On the night-rock
Dragged words from my lips
But the white sea wave
And winter wind cut
All verbs I called
Until in silence I returned
To my path treading shadow
Cast by the moon on the road
I walk.

My first song was for the sea
(to ease my fear), no cathedral,
No odyssey, no spectral love.
The alphabet I played
Was a syllable for death.
And having sung in silence
To night-breakers by the shore
I saw the moon turn tail
And disappear.

5

I followed a black hag winding
Through halls of distorting glass
And knew at last that only by a token
Between each heart
Is there chain enough to bind
A love and life
On blazing rock where eyes deceive.

6

And only words called each to each
Are tokens, from one skull to another,
Holding vigil beneath the skin
As a vacant shell and mask
Is circling and aloud with stars.

I call.   I call.
My pulse is requiem
That must salve wounds
I cannot bind
Until I hear a hymn
From the white rose
As I pass by your summer grave.

Five songs
Moonsong

Rise through the sky
To the moon way above
I spin on my couch
From this Earth that I love.

O I will walk
On the grey tranquil sea
Casting no shadow
Seeking no mystery.

I'll gather dust
And some diamond rock
To give blue Earth
For her jealous stock.

Don't look for me
Singing over your head
Join the moonsong
And our freefalling tread.

Orpheus is here
In gold tinted dome,
Icarus left
On his long way home.

We have marked the track
Through orbital bar
And sung our way
To this lonely star.

These five songs are sung by Mike Campbell-Cole to his own music and guitar accompaniment.

Now raise your eyes
And your voice and your hands
The moon has danced
To Apollo's band.

O rise through space
To the stars way above
Spin on your couches
From the blue Earth you love.

Song of the Wind
For Michael Campbell-Cole

I will accompany the wind
Over mountain
And through gold field:
I will tease spray
From tall wave crest.
O I will accompany the wind.

Riding a song
In every ear:
Among city street
In lonely room,
I will accompany the wind.

O I will accompany the wind
Until the chain
Of my white bones
Drifts like fine sand
And I become compassing wind.

And I become the wind.

Liberty Track

O cry me farewell
My Liberty Track
I watch from my cell but
You ain't coming back.

I once used to say
I'd take me to town,
Drink my release pay
And tuck with a gown.

Met with a fast girl
And broke my parole.
Now count off my whirl
Breaking Liberty's soul.

Break me a quarry
Remission's all gone.
Goddam the jury,
Ten days number one.

Take her and keep her
And dress her in rust,
Send her some flowers
She's all that I trust.

O cry me farewell
My Liberty Track
I watch from my cell but
You ain't coming back.

Mountains Sing

Mountains sing and oceans whistle.
What wife weaves one coloured cotton?
And say what woodsman clips from one tree;
Not me.

I took a rose while walking
And the bee lost his honey.
He had three,
O he had three,
But the bee lost his honey.

And now there are two stings
in me
And now there are two stings
in me.

My Love come and join Me

My love come and join me
The water is fine.
Bricks and mortar
Rot in time.

Summer is through
I've got no place to go.
Leaves are falling
I've got no dough.

Work isn't for me,
Tea's to my taste.
Where have you been
Through dreams I chased?

My love come and join me
The water is fine.
Bricks and mortar
Rot in time.

Cities are crowded
So I'll have to go
Where there are no doors
And the wind can blow.

I can't bear traffic,
Tarmac's too hard,
Must find me a hill
With no backyard.

My love come and join me
The water is fine.
Bricks and mortar
Rot in time.

The Anchorage

The anchorage is scored by down
Drawn wind. An old trawler holds
Against tide and current while around
Her a fleck of gulls colour dark water
And her iron hull. On the welldeck
A fisherman cleans the fish haul
Throwing entrails to impatient
Birds buffeting each other
Over the full larder of the sea.

The trawler turns to the tide
And her lights double on reflection.
The wind drops and across the bay
Drum of lapping water rythmns
Against her hull.   On the cliff
By Marisco Castle the cottage lights
Repeat the theme reflected in eyes
On shore, in the dreaming stare
Of the moon in the anchorage.

The sound of a fisherman on the ship
Rasps into night before the first
Fingers of a rising wind
Begin to play with tune and light down
The long water and fugue of the sea.

Wendy Anne Mitchell

> *'Wendy Anne Mitchell,*
> *Poet, aged 21,*
> *Who died on Lundy,*
> *9th July 1952.'*

I stand on the cliff's edge
Overlooking Halftide Rock
Down a searoad to the Atlantic.

In my ears a moaning psalm
Peels from Rock Island
Echoed by basking seal,

And I feel the hand
Of the virgin poet touch mine
As she falls again and again

Onto the calling rocks
That are the Eastern portals
Of the ocean where she is poet

Of 'the paradise that only we
The young and proud may know.'

Lines from Wales
For Kit Barker

Farewell.
  My room has cracked walls
which trace fantasies and fables
  as I lie abed.

Farewell.
  A hurt part of my nerves
beneath an abused eiderdown
  moves in the darkness.

Farewell.
  The straw I stretch under
and flint I elbow, consume,
  and amuse me.

Farewell.
  O Oblomov, salute –
Shield against sawbladed morning,
  pull the curtains closed –

Farewell.
  Until this volcanic
head shakes out the coals and madness
  Of Porthos Barsac.

Elan Valley
For Kit and Ilse

Hide of cattle, feather of fowl,
Granite of hill and wild mountain,
Lonely, lonely, lovely Elan.

To see, to live, is to be breath
On ice, tear in a storm of rain: is man
Among autumn rising in your long voice.

At the Glen of Drumtochty
For George and Elspeth

An eagle spans the Glen of Drumtochty,
Three deerhounds lope across the hills.
I dream a pace behind the oldest dog
Along a track up through the Glen
While a babel of leaves and wind
Flaunt my voice which I keep silent
Until a jet howls along the tunnel-sky
Passing out of eye and ear in a gasp,
Leaving the Glen echoing with a laugh
I did not hear but know came from my lips.

The eagle hovers and the deerhounds grace;
Granite sinks a fraction into the hill.
Tall fir trees cushion the slope,
Hares curvet, even the river
Is barely moving through the Glen
As I sit on a rock and look down, down
Into the dream kingdom of Drumtochty.

An eagle is above me – sun and moon,
And the deerhounds sit like three grey monarchs.
The world stopped for a moment, held transfixed,
Until as though a gulliver breathing
Drumtochty moved.

An eagle wheeled over a crag
Deerhound nudged me, tree became tree,
River fell over rock and shrilled.
Again the jet rasped overhead
And I walked a world away from the oldest hound
Along the pathway down into the Glen.

The Zennor Road
For G. B.

Late and the getting later moon calls
After a poet who grabs at the sky
And on his knees, stumbling drunk,
Prays for Li Po's immortal soul.

April Mooned

I walk towards the moon
Sliding on lakes of light
Among April trees, and step on
Stretched gates printed bright.

On the road I mooned home
I read the pages of the sky,
Silent of birds, understanding some,
As with a long and lazy eye

I flipped the punctuation
Of stars, and was flummoxed
By lying creation
That leads to a pine box.

Beyond Astronaut

And out in the black chart
Of lightlives away ride the roaring
Boys who slide through space.

A universe of unmapped grief and love
And new master light is beyond
The pleiades and plough and southern stars.
Far sisters far behind, left standing
As lean lads gyrate, siren
Silent, through the bewildering sky.
See them take a superstition which makes
Endless the forever night of destiny
Beyond sight and measure.

                O soaring
Icarus of outworld, burn bright
The traceries of known skymarks,
Slide the highway planets behind
Your clear waxed wings.

Go conquer the everywhere left
Beyond your sad confinement
In a predicted bonehouse,
Witch thrown riddle of flesh
And water.

             O soar until nothing
Remains but great glittering holes
In the black godspun shirt over your head.

Columbus of the Sky

Riding discovery a moonbeam
Behind night, polka-dot sky,
I find the eggstand crushed
In a rivalry of ships below
All horizons.

      O pilot pearled
On a trident wail and preach
A prayer for each confused king
Crucified on your beaches.
Sit on a throne worn thin by tears,
Risk those highways out of sight
Crawling with diamond disaster:
Dominions Alexander axed
in mind.

      O rider soar rocket
Round creation out of eyes
Away from the window where we are
Mouthing who gave us the right
To own a universe.   Go find
Your kingdoms and your grave.
Break me a nightmare hacked to death
Whose bit is between her skies,

Sound archipelagoes of the air,
Beat round the storming planets
And map a geography of space.

The Sea of Tranquillity
For John Moat

The sinews tighten as my head tilts back
To look at the sky; in particular the moon.
My eyes travel through the peels of Space
To those ancient bodies that might still be:
Although the moment I see started so long ago
That the light reflected in my eyes is older
That my mind will calendar.

                Now I
Hold with the bits of metal we throw up
Ranging orbits farther out each chance.
I watch the stars and divine weary Magi
With spinning gifts in foam-fitting couches;
And my voice is loud in the night and calls the capsules
In from their fragile hour on the Tranquil Sea.

It is the moon and Space we speak of vaguely,
But the voice and eye and hand and metal
Is born and raised on heartbreak and pigliver,
Mashed potatoes and physics, tact and fiction.

I salute the electric wheels of memory,
The bobbing piston, and assembly line, the can
Of beer and pack of frozen beans. I cheer
The halting metal eggs that orbit earth
One manned or three.

                I acclaim supermarket
And paperbacks, the T.V. and the stratojet.
My eyes are full of stars; and the moon-dust
Is settling over Cape Kennedy for the next count
Which I echo in my heart.

                Cosmonaut stretch out
A hand towards a friend and speak fearlessly.
The battle is engaged against friction and bloodpushing 'G'.

The arrows, bullets, dungeons, tortures, are in the eyes
Nearer than the light reflected when the sinews
Tighten as my head is thrown back to scan the moon.
The moon is no longer the same.   No longer the same.

Blue moon – harvest moon – lover's moon – man in the moon
Is superseded as of 20th February, 1965,
When Ranger Eight broke its back on a grey sea,
The Mare Tranquillitatis, and raised dust
That didn't get itself spat on and rolled
Into, harrowed, ploughed, sandcastled. The moon is different.

It now stares down with a foreign body
Like a thorn splinter just beneath the skin,
And a future likely to trick the past.

Old man, O moon, I saw you before the instrument
Pierced you, and I see you now.   I almost feel the same
And honestly cannot decry your violation.
We are both different now, you and I.

          I'm long glad
I don't have to ride a horse, saddle a brute;
But can tune twin-carbs and howl down a Clearway
When and where I wish as quickly as I choose.

The more there is around and on you, moon, the more
I speculate on machines and computers and am pleased
And grateful.   It makes history an evolution.
And those fitting who had a hand in putting
The Eighth Ranger into the depthless dustful sea.
It makes the nails and lives and compassion and hero and coward
And God and tomb-robber, judged and judge,
The whole crazy unbalance of recorded man
A small piece of expensive engineering, dust covered,
On a coagulated gas we moon.

          Moon that nights
And shows us where to put drunken feet
As we stagger from fire-sides to throw
Our heads back until the sinews in our necks tighten
And beneath our feet the orb is reflected
In a river we can touch: We can touch and embrace.

Space Walk

Around, around in freefall thought
The clinging cosmo-astronaut,

Awkward and expensive star
Dogpaddles from his spinning car.

Makes the dark and vacant place
A refuge for the unshaved face.

Look up my friend and note it well
This orbit where food packets dwell.

Thought's the same in black and white,
Cave figures jump in candlelight.

Hang on man buckled to your egg;
You're off your knees.   No longer beg.

It doesn't matter who you are
The highway coming is a star.

Cosmo-astronaut in space
Your anchor cord our act of grace.

12 Stations from Gemini

1

Dials indicate fable
Exploding
This shell into orbit.

Hand, eye, and tongue record
The spinning
Guess that is destiny.

2

Earth and sun, sun and earth
Pull me to
Them in quickening beauty.

From cave to capsule I
Swim weightless
To generate a star.

3

The long, long haul is on
Across void
Out into unthinkable

Space where men pursue
The anger
Of their image into gods.

4

I awake to the gold
Tint of light
That is my emblemed shield.

Gold shield, gold cord, anchor
Me to life
And precise blind gauges.

5

Around, up, forward, turn;
Movements call
Mind and blood, counting steps

That I take looking back
Along skies
That curve to forever.

6

Endlessly you and I
Move from or
To our deaths and issue.

Who will inherit stars?
My dust and
Theirs? Where, where are you?

7

This suit is not my skin,
This vein does
Not throb with my blood,

These teeth and nails will fall.
My eyes fail
In this golden vizor.

8

Yet I am here and proud.
O the awe
The wonderful threshold

Turning, turning away
In distances
My heart and mind will cross.

9

Do not build me a tomb,
Cast medal,
Or call streets by my name.

Out here memorial
Is nothing: dust
That collects about my head.

10

It is easier to
Withstand G
Than the piledriving death

That comes from remaining
Unarmed and
Afraid of changing stars.

11

Roaring towards nothing
But distant
Holes and wilder guesses

I'll lie here cramped, singing
To you who
Are deaf to the calling sky.

12

For if stories are false
I'm with gods
Who either care or do not

Who or why or what I am,
And where I
Spin my stations for you.

Adrift on the Star Brow of Taliesin

My beginning is the dominion of stars,
A spinning bell gave me tongue
To sing through peels of space.

I am the black tide of your blood,
I am the white waves of your mind,
I am the magnet of your bones.

There is no shape to my body.
No cold nor heat touches my skin,
No song nor algebra escapes my brain.

For you I sing through broken crust
Of one blue earth, and thread distances
With an energy you expel.

—

I was conceived in lost cave
Where flame spoke to damp rock.

I was in the desert for days
Endlessly exercising colour.

I was the first sound on tongue,
First curse to kill.

The first stone thrown in anger
First blood leaking life.

I gleaned ears of wild corn
I rode seas on leaf and log.

I filled castle and hovel
Cowshed and nook chanting

Words of innocence in wine,
Words of love in blood.

I starved among pearls,
I turned the screw on the wheel.

I grew nails through my hands,
I grew thorns on my forehead.

I heard voices in the wind,
Heard echoes in the rock.

—

Through nine months of history
I crouched in shadow
Listening to blood whispering.
As I turned towards the tunnel
Of birth I rode an endless
Breaker of blood to pitch
On a strand of life and death.

—

While there is a word to be said
By one man to another I will
Cross from mouth to mouth.
I will cast my shadow along
The trajectory of birth
And tears, and chant a lullaby
To myself with words for you.

Throw stones at me
And I will simply change
Into a wall – or die
For a moment.
Through a labyrinth
Of rhyme the poets
Move from grove
To grave until the chain
Of their voices loop
The farthest star
To spill germs of you and me
In endless flight and song.

—

I have been in flight forever,
Long before man staggered to his feet.
I curl now in the spinning womb
Listening to nerve twitching
Of computers and dials
And sing to myself within the shell
As I wait to burst
Into the first intaken breath
Of an infant smacked to life
By a hand that soothes
Pain from the starways of disbelief.

I move on when I know my song
Has passed from the hand to the infant,
So the calling tongue and word
Has no distance between this spinning
Shell and the spirals of space.

—

Into unthinkable uncountable
Tomorrow I must move
Carrying the knot, and cast of spells,
And love and hate, death and birth,
And metaphysics of guessing
From each grave to each cot
From each womb to each tongue.
There must be no break in the circle
While the word is sung
And while new stars are added
To the fantasy of maps.

—

I cut the cord between idea
And formula and then tune a lullaby
Or lament into words to tease
Understanding, to brave the slings
Of fear and pride, to circumvent
A pit of seething words
That dissolve into a swamp
Of personal myth.

—

I speak of these things
Because I want you to know
That although I am away
From here – passed the eye
That reads – yet I am
Circling from the brow
Of Taliesin.

—

In winter frost and wind
I send a tune so loud
It cannot be heard
Unless the ear is tuned
Beyond listening.

With Spring I am the leap
Of salmon and explosion
In the legs of March hare.

In Summer I am the haze
Over lake and river,
I ride the tip of swallow tail
And dance on butterfly wing.

In Autumn I am the last fruit,
I am evening fog and sharp air,
I am the log hissing in ember.

All. All these. I am all blood
That is running, all bones
And hearts that are broken
By the truncheon of seasons.

—

Always I circle in a vessel
Of tomorrow bursting on dust
So infertile that only wilderness
Can couple with the flood of energy
That requires you to follow me
Adrift here among the stars.

By the same Author

Books of Verse
This I Say
The 5th Horseman of the Apocalypse
Adrift on the Star Brow of Taliesin

Edited Anthologies
Listen to This
Stop and Listen
Double Image
Horizons
Frontier of Going

Prose
Concorde File

Edited
Literary magazine: Nimbus
Guest Editor: Southern Arts Literary Supplement
London Editor: Panache (N.Y.)
Poetry Editor: Resurgence

Adrift on the Star Brow of Taliesin
". . . is an attempt to create a poetry that can encompass man's coming-of-age, and the Taliesin figure becomes something like the principle of human imagination.
The aim is to confront a cyclical creatorless universe and out of that confrontation to reaffirm the imagination's values.
Fairfax's strongest moments tend to come back at his starting point, in his sense of man's harmony with and yet isolation within nature, and his refusal in the face of difficulty to accede to any myth, religious or political."

London Magazine

The 5th Horseman of the Apocalypse
". . . The imagery beautifully echoes a scientific age facing the holocaust . . . an incantation and a narrative witness, showing a fierce imagination never undermined by despair or by elemental reality."

Southern Arts Review